YOU CAN

have an outdoor adventure

Alex Gregory

CONTENTS

YOU CAN HAVE AN OUTDOOR ADVENTURE

Having an outdoor adventure is really easy! This book will give you loads of inspiration so that YOU CAN go and have your very own adventures.

Open your front door, breathe in the fresh air, and prepare yourself for lots of fun! This book is full of activities that you can do in your own back garden, and other activities that will take you further away from home – outdoor adventures can be had everywhere!

There is something for everyone – whether you want to climb a tree, make leaf prints to hang on your bedroom wall, create a hotel for busy bees, go stargazing or rock pooling, or feast on banana pancakes.

There are also plenty of spaces in the book for you to jot down what you've found, draw what you've seen and record the details of your adventures.
So what are you waiting for? Read on, and then go and have an outdoor adventure!

Don't forget, whenever you're off on an outdoor adventure, it's really important to have a grown-up with you, especially when...

✹ ...you're climbing

✹ ...using sharp tools like knives, scissors, and bows and arrows

✹ ...making fires

✹ ...getting close to wildlife

✹ ...you're sleeping outside

✹ ...you're in and around water

✹ ...you're foraging – and cooking and eating food you've foraged.

TREES

Trees are the lungs to our world and everything living on it. It's difficult to explain just how important trees are and often we forget. It's important that everyone in the world cares for trees, protects them, helps them and grows them themselves.

Trees can be found everywhere, from the countryside to the city, from the national parks to the town centres, but one thing is for sure, there are nowhere near enough trees in this world.

Why not go outside and learn to identify some trees? When you start knowing what it is you're looking at, it's easier to care. At the right time of year, you can even find some seeds and have a go at growing your own!

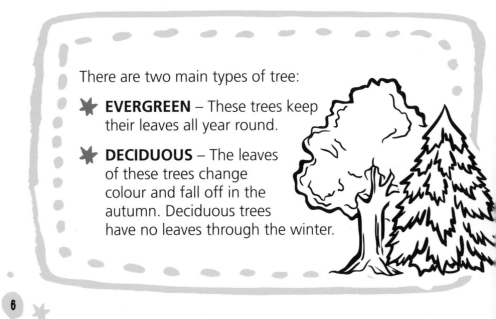

There are two main types of tree:

* **EVERGREEN** – These trees keep their leaves all year round.

* **DECIDUOUS** – The leaves of these trees change colour and fall off in the autumn. Deciduous trees have no leaves through the winter.

There are about 60,000 different species of amazing trees in the world. Here are some of the most common trees:

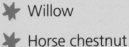

- ⭐ Beech
- ⭐ Oak
- ⭐ Hawthorn
- ⭐ Hazel

- ⭐ Silver birch
- ⭐ Willow
- ⭐ Horse chestnut
- ⭐ Sycamore

Find a leaf from each type of tree!

Do you know which trees these seeds come from?

1

2

3

Answers: 1. Oak; 2. Horse chestnut; 3. Sycamore

GROW A TREE

At the right time of year, you can do something to improve the environment in which you live. Trees are great things to have near you for so many reasons. They are good to look at, to touch, to draw, to watch grow, to care for, to provide a habitat (place to live) for other things to live on, and to clean up the air around you.

In late summer and early autumn when the leaves are changing colour on the trees, head outside on a mission – it's time to go searching for tree seeds!

TREE SEEDS

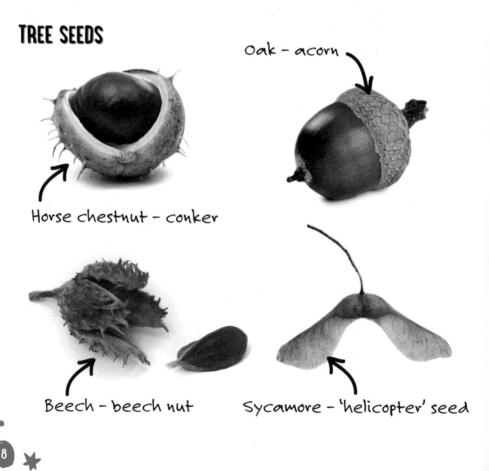

Oak – acorn

Horse chestnut – conker

Beech – beech nut

Sycamore – 'helicopter' seed

Here is how you can grow a tree from a tree seed!

What to do

1 Fill the container with soil. Make sure there are some small drainage holes in the bottom of the container.

2 Push the seed carefully into the soil and cover it with loose soil.

3 Water the seed well.

4 Place in a warm, light position, and wait.

5 Check regularly to ensure the soil is damp, not wet. Eventually you will see the first shoot of your tree!

You'll need:

* a tree seed

* a container – this could be an empty milk carton, a plant pot, plastic bottle or any similar container

* soil – a pile of soil from the garden or compost from a shop, enough to fill your container

* water – a few drops to get the seed growing!

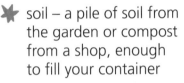

It will take quite a while for the first shoot to appear. You will need to be patient, but eventually you'll be rewarded with your very own tree.

You will be able to keep your tree in a plant pot outdoors for many years once it has started to establish itself. One day you will be able to plant it out in your garden, but for now enjoy moving it into different positions so you can see it and remind yourself of the importance of trees.

TREE CLIMBING

Everyone loves climbing trees. Sometimes grown-ups pretend they don't but usually, when they do climb, they end up laughing, smiling, and having a whole load of fun! That's what tree climbing is for, having fun, but it's also really good for you. Make sure you've got an adult with you when you are climbing.

Climbing trees teaches you loads of stuff that is quite difficult to learn in other places. It's a challenge that involves thought, balance and strength. Knowing different species and how they grow is important because this can tell you which trees are good for climbing and which are not. Tree climbing isn't always about climbing high. Even a small distance off the ground counts and can be just as fun!

When you're climbing a tree, you are:

* getting fitter and stronger
* learning how to climb safely
* discovering a world that many people never get to see
* seeing the world from a different point of view
* getting huge benefit from being in touch with nature
* breathing fresh air
* having an adventure that you can write and talk about!

Which trees have you climbed?

Plane   ☐

Horse chestnut   ☐

Oak   ☐

Ash   ☐

Beech   ☐

Other   ☐

What did you see when you were in the tree?
Draw it here.

LEAF PRINTS

Nature is the most perfect artist. The incredible beauty that nature creates never fails to amaze, as long as you take the time to look.

You can use nature as a helping hand to create something very special. If you pick up a leaf from the floor, look closely at its features: colours, veins, shape, structure and texture. You can use these details to make your own amazing art.

What to do

1 Take this book outside and collect a range of different leaves.

2 Once you're back home, very carefully paint the surface of the leaves, one leaf at a time. It's better to use a thin layer of paint on each leaf.

3 Press the painted leaf paint-side down onto some paper then pull off immediately. Hopefully you'll see the leaf printed onto the paper!

4 Repeat this process with all the leaves.

5 You can create a picture, different patterns, simple designs – there are so many options!

6 How about creating your own leaf print guide? Print the leaf of a tree and write information about the tree next to it – you can create your very own identification book.

⭐ Leaves are food factories for trees and plants. Without leaves, trees wouldn't live and grow.

⭐ The green colour in leaves is called chlorophyll and sucks in a gas called carbon dioxide from the air. Chlorophyll uses water that the tree has sucked up from the ground and the carbon dioxide in the leaf to make special sugars. This is the tree's food and helps it grow. This process is called photosynthesis.

⭐ Deciduous trees drop their leaves in winter.

⭐ Evergreen trees stay green all through the year.

⭐ You can use trees to help you work out which way you're pointing: north, south, east or west (see page 83).

FIRES

Fires can be dangerous. Fires can be scary. Fires can be a lot of fun!

Learning how to light a fire is a great skill (make sure you always have an adult with you though). It's a challenge but is a useful one to master and is so satisfying when you manage it. Once you learn the basics, you'll always have the skills and be the one that everyone calls on to get the fire going!

Fires changed the path of human civilisation. The earliest people around 1 million years ago could begin to cook the food they ate, protect themselves from dangerous predators and keep themselves warmer. This meant they could travel to colder places in the world and survive. Over time, many people have lost these skills. Let's try to bring them back!

Fires need a few things to work.

TINDER – some very dry material that lights easily. Dry fibres are ideal.

KINDLING – small, thin, dry wood that catches alight easily.

FUEL – wood is what keeps a fire going. It's what burns for long periods of time and really creates the heat.

A SPARK – this is the part that no fire can do without. You can make sparks in different ways and it's great fun trying different methods. The simplest way is to use a match.

START YOUR OWN FIRE

It's useful to be able to spot the suitable things to get a fire lit and burning well. Tinder is the first part of any fire, so head outside and see how many suitable materials you can find. List them here. Each time you go out, you can add to the list.

Tinder list

DID YOU KNOW?

Some people store suitable tinder material under their clothes to dry it out, so it's perfect for later when they need to get the fire going… What do you think about doing this?!

Here is how you can start a fire.

What to do

Make sure an adult is present every time you do anything involving fire.

1 Find a suitable place to light a fire. This must be outdoors, away from buildings, fences or anything that could catch alight.

2 Prepare a pile of tinder, kindling and fuel, and have your spark maker ready to go.

3 Light your tinder by touching a spark onto its fibres.

4 Quickly add very small, thin, dry pieces of kindling, allowing it to catch alight.

5 Build up the amount of kindling you add until it's well-lit and flames have established themselves.

6 Add the fuel on top carefully, making sure you don't smother the fire and put it out.

7 Take every step carefully. Don't rush but be quick enough to make sure that each stage works.

8 Fires are difficult to get right every time. Be patient, and if a stage doesn't work first time, don't worry. Start again and build up each stage slowly.

9 If it ever looks like the flame is going to go out, blow very gently to give the fire oxygen, which it needs to burn!

Once you have built up the heat of the fire with each stage, you'll be able to keep adding fuel to maintain the heat and keep the fire going.

BE SAFE!

Always stay with your fire. Never leave a fire unattended.

THE QUICKEST FIRE

Sometimes you just need a really quick fire on your adventures to warm you up if you're cold, and dry you off if you're wet, or to make a hot chocolate when you're in need of some energy! In those times you might just need a little helping hand.

What to do

1 With an adult's help, carefully light a fire lighter and gently pile the kindling over the top, allowing it to catch light.

2 The fire lighter replaces tinder. It's designed to be easy to light even in wet conditions and stays alight for a long time, giving you time to build your fire.

3 Once the kindling is well-lit, start slowly adding fuel, making sure not to smother the fire!

You'll need:

✸ fire lighters

✸ matches

✸ kindling

✸ fuel

BE SAFE!

While fires can be lots of fun, they can also be dangerous, so make sure you always have an adult with you.

This is an easy way to light a fire quickly. You still need to be prepared, but in a rush this is a good method. Once you have your fire going, you can boil your water in a metal pan or kettle and have your lovely warm adventure drink!

FIRE LIGHTERS

There are different types of fire lighters. Always get the eco versions that are simply wood fibres and wax, rather than being full of chemicals. They are environmentally friendly and easy to find online.

FIRE CHALLENGE

A fun challenge is to have a super small fire! Being able to light and control a tiny fire is a real skill. Once a fire is going, it's so easy to make it BIGGER. Keeping it small is much more of a challenge and sometimes more fun!

You'll need:

kindling

fuel

metal snips

tin can

tinder

What to do

1 Get an adult to cut small holes in the bottom of the can using the metal snips. This is to allow the intake of air.

2 Place the can outside, on a stable, flat surface or the ground.

3 Light the tinder in the bottom of the tin can and carefully add kindling from the top or through the holes.

4 Keep the fire going by adding fuel through the tin can opening.

5 See how long you can keep your tin can fire going!

BE SAFE!

The tin can will get extremely hot!
Do not touch the can while the fire is lit.

Because the fire is so small, the chance of the fuel burning out quickly is very high. This means you must be aware of any changes that you have to make. This challenge involves observation, thought, skill, care and patience. Have fun!

CHARCOAL DRAWING

Once you're finished with your fire, whatever type you choose to have, keep an eye out for any half-burnt sticks or twigs. Keep these for some charcoal art!

Charcoal is wood that has been burnt without much oxygen. It's excellent to use for drawing.

What to do

1 Make sure any pieces of charcoal are completely cold and are unlit.

2 Pick up the charcoal and use it as a pen or pencil! Charcoal art is a fantastic way of creating something really special.

3 Why not draw something you can see, like the fire you've just had? Or try something from your imagination!

4 Each time you have a fire, collect a few pieces of charcoal to add to a charcoal pencil case!

Have a go at your own charcoal drawing here.

BOW AND ARROW

Do you know the story of Robin Hood? Now's your chance to be Robin Hood on one of your outdoor adventures! Robin's weapon of choice was the trusty bow and arrow. Nowadays they aren't weapons, they are actually used in the Olympics in archery. In competition they use high-tech bows and arrows, but you can make them out of wood.

What to do

1 Using a penknife, very carefully remove any twigs or leaves from both of your sticks. Ask an adult to help you with this.

2 Carefully cut a small notch 1 cm from each end of the hazel wood stick.

3 Tie the string to both ends very tightly, making sure the hazel wood stick is bent slightly by the tight string.

4 Carefully carve a point in the shorter arrow stick.

5 Cut a small notch at the other end that will hold onto the string.

6 With an adult, and in an open space, practise firing your arrow. Practise distance and accuracy. Never point an arrow at another person.

You'll need:

* a hazel wood stick at least 1 m long
* strong string
* a penknife
* a thin, very straight stick, around 50 cm long

Try making a bow out of other types of wood. Are some types of wood better than others? Which wood is good for bows and which wood is bad?

Wood type	Good/Bad?	Why?

WILDLIFE

Have you ever seen...

...a fox slinking through a hedgerow?

...a tawny owl flying silently above your head?

...a hunting pike?

...a mole sticking its head out of the ground?

All these things and so much more are happening every day, and most people have no idea. It's all out there – you just need to get outside, be patient and look.

There are ways to encourage amazing creatures to come to you. Sometimes it's the tiny things happening right under your feet that are the most amazing of all. Discovering them is an adventure in itself!

When you go outside make a note of any creatures you see.

Date seen	Species	Description

BUG HUNT

If you head outside and look – I mean really look – you will find bugs, insects and other creepy crawlies. They are absolutely everywhere and actually, humans rely on them in order to survive!

Have you ever looked closely at one? They are so weird and wonderful it's hard to believe they exist. If you took a really close-up picture (macro image), you may well think they were aliens from outer space.

They help humans in so many different ways. They break down waste, and pollinate plants, flowers and trees – including the plants you eat. They provide food for other creatures, which keeps them alive, and they probably do so much more that you don't even know about! Bugs are super important, so take a moment to appreciate them!

lesser stag beetle

Which creepy crawlies do you already know?
Tick the box if you've seen one and write its
name on the line underneath.

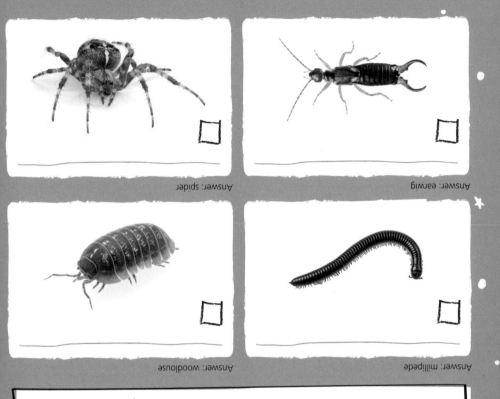

Answer: spider

Answer: earwig

Answer: woodlouse

Answer: millipede

There's some space to draw and label your own here.

BUGS UP CLOSE

It's easy to make a bug trap. This won't harm the creatures but will allow you to collect some and look closely at them.

What to do

1 Dig a hole as deep as the container.

2 Place the container in the hole, making sure the top of it is level with the surface of the ground.

3 Drop the bait in the container.

4 Place two rocks on either side of the container in the ground and place the flat rock (the 'lid') on top. Leave a bit of space for the creepy crawlies to get in.

5 The trap is set!

6 Leave the trap all day or overnight. When you come to check the trap, you're sure to have a whole load of tiny creatures to study.

7 Carefully pull out the container and see what you've caught.

8 When you've finished studying them, remember to let them go.

You'll need:

* a cup / container with steep sides

* a spade / trowel

* three rocks, one bigger and flatter than the other two

* food scraps / bait

TIP!

Pour your newly caught bugs into a glass or jar. You will be able to look at them closely through the glass.

Now study your bugs. In the box below, draw them, write about them or stick in a photo. You could use an identification book to help you.

DRAWING CREEPY CRAWLIES

Here are some really simple steps to follow that will create some brilliant results!

HOW TO DRAW A WOODLOUSE

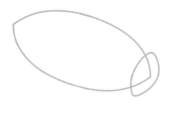

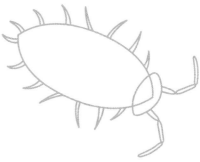

1 Start by drawing a big oval for the body and a small oval for the head.

2 Add 14 legs and 2 antennae.

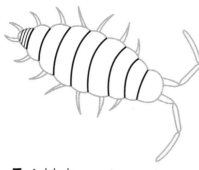

3 Add shapes to create segments on the body.

4 Add some detail and you're done!

HOW TO DRAW A SPIDER

1 Start by drawing an oval
for the body and a circle
for the head.

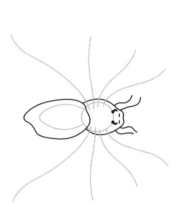

2 Add 8 lines for the
spider's 8 legs.

3 Make an outline for the
head and body, and add
eyes and features.

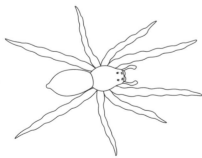

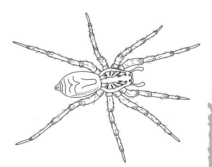

4 Draw the legs around
the guide lines you drew
in step 2.

5 Finish by adding a spider
pattern to the body and
hairs on the legs.

IDENTIFICATION BOOK

Use the steps on the previous page to draw your own spiders and woodlice. You can draw other creatures too and make your very own identification book!

TRACKING WILDLIFE

People have been tracking wildlife forever. It's one of the skills that has meant people have been able to find food right through history. Why not give it a go while out on one of your adventures and see how close you can get to the wildlife?

Animals often use the same route to get to where they want to go – from their home to a favourite feeding ground, for example. Along these paths you may find a combination of clues that tell you exactly what is there.

FOOTPRINTS

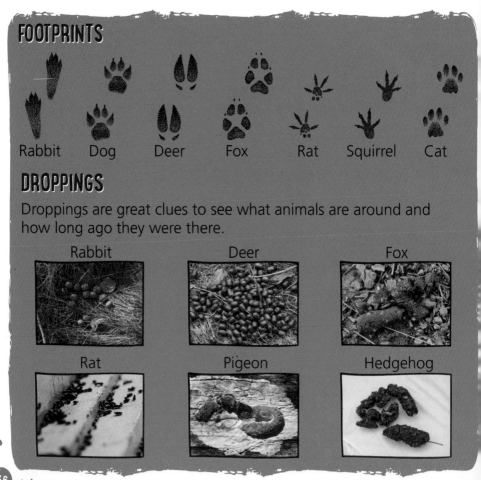

Rabbit   Dog   Deer   Fox   Rat   Squirrel   Cat

DROPPINGS

Droppings are great clues to see what animals are around and how long ago they were there.

Rabbit   Deer   Fox

Rat   Pigeon   Hedgehog

FUR

Hair or fur caught in bushes or on fences can give a really good clue about the animal you're tracking.

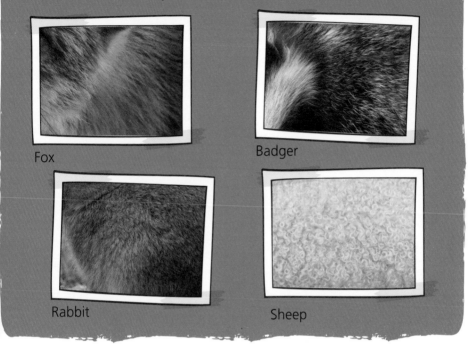

Fox

Badger

Rabbit

Sheep

What did you see?

Footprints	Fur	Droppings	Other	What is the animal?

BAT DETECTING

When the sun is going down and it's getting dark, it's usually time to go indoors. The trouble is, you're missing out on some really amazing adventures! Dusk is the time that bats come out to feed and there's something very special about being outside with bats flying around you!

What to do

1 Bats really enjoy feeding near water, so if you have a pond in your garden or near you, that's the best place to start.

2 As it starts to get dark, keep your eyes peeled. Bats are super quick and agile, and really difficult to spot, but when you do, you'll know!

3 If you have a bat detector, turn it on and listen for the sounds that the bats are making. This sound is called echolocation and is the bat's way of hunting.

You'll need:

✳ a bat detector (ask a grown-up if they can help you buy one online)

or

✳ just keep your eyes peeled

4 With the bat detector you will be able to tell when they are near, and often how many there are. It gives you a picture of sound and it really is so exciting!

5 Bats are really difficult to identify because they move so quickly in low light that you can't really see them. One way is to listen to their sound with the bat detector, because each one sounds slightly different.

Go outside with a grown-up every evening for a week in summer and see how many bats you can count.

	Day 1	Day 2	Day 3	Day 4	Day 5	Day 6	Day 7
Number of bats							

Did the number of bats vary? What do you think affected the numbers?

BAT FACTS

* The tiny pipistrelle bat weighs the same as a 20p piece!
* Pipistrelle bats can eat up to 3000 tiny insects in one night!

pipistrelle bat

BEE HOTEL

It's so important to look after the wildlife around us. This hasn't always been done, but thankfully now more and more people are wanting to help! Without wildlife you wouldn't be able to have nearly as many adventures, so do your bit and help creatures when you can.

Have you ever thought about giving bees a helping hand by building them a five-star luxury hotel?

What to do

You'll need:

* an old plant pot with a hole in the bottom
* a spade or trowel
* dry grass / straw

1 Find a quiet spot in the garden that won't get disturbed – under a hedge or in a flower bed would be perfect.

2 Dig a hole nearly as big as the plant pot.

3 Fill the hole with the grass or straw.

4 Place the plant pot upside down into the hole, covering the grass or straw. Make sure you put the pot in at an angle so the hole points more towards you, not straight upwards.

5 Fill in the soil around the edges.

6 Now wait for a bee to find its new home!

Draw the bee hotel you've made.

Remember! Other creepy crawlies like beetles and spiders will make their way into this hotel and make their home there. This is OK. Hopefully one day a bee will find it, but if not, you're giving a helping hand to other important wild creatures!

BIRD FEEDER

Some wildlife needs more help than others, and birds definitely need help. It's really easy to make a big difference to birds by feeding them.

Have you ever made a bird feeder?

What to do

1 Ask a grown-up to carefully pierce a hole near the bottom of the bottle using scissors, and do the same directly opposite the first hole.

2 Repeat that process until there are 4 holes in the bottle.

3 Push the sticks through the holes. These will be perches for the birds when they come to feed.

4 Now, about 4 cm above each perch, cut a small hole in the bottle that will be the opening for the birds to get to the seeds.

5 Tie some string around the top of the bottle, just under the place where the lid screws on, to create a loop.

6 Open the bottle lid and fill it with bird seed.

7 Hang your new bird feeder in a tree and wait for the birds to come for dinner!

You'll need:

* a clean, washed plastic bottle
* two thin, straight sticks
* a small pair of scissors
* some string
* bird seed

How about heading out in search of rubbish, including a plastic bottle to use as your bird feeder? Take a bag and go on a litter collecting adventure. See how quickly you can fill up your bag – make sure you wear gloves!

If you picked up plastic bottles from the ground, you've done a fantastic job at clearing up the environment. You've turned rubbish into a bird feeder, recycled a bottle and done some real good for the bird population. Now you can enjoy watching what birds your feeder attracts!

Note down what birds you see eating from your bird feeder.

Bird type (species)	Date seen

UNDER THE STARS

Have you ever spent time outside under the stars? Some people are unsure about the darkness, a little nervous perhaps. That's okay – if you're not used to it, it's completely understandable. Night-time can be amazing though. You can see, hear and do unusual things and have some brilliant adventures!

Each day, it goes dark at a different time. It might only change by a minute or two, but it will change.

Fill in the table once a week to keep track of what time it goes dark and see if you notice a pattern!

	Week 1	Week 2	Week 3	Week 4	Week 5	Week 6	Week 7
What time did it go dark?							

Night-time feels completely different to day-time. A place you know well can feel like a totally different world. It's when the stars come out and you'll notice that every night the moon is a different shape. Animals you don't see in the daylight come out, and often, if you don't see them, you'll hear them instead. It's a mysterious time that everyone should experience and get to enjoy.

A NIGHT-TIME WALK

Why not go outside when you should be asleep? This is an exciting thing to do but you may have to wait for the weekend or a school holiday to go. Always remember to take an adult with you.

Wrap up warm, go out of the door and start your night-time adventure!

What to do

Take a torch with you, but it's best to try and walk with it turned off. Very quickly, your eyes will adjust, and you'll be amazed at how much you can actually see in the dark. Notice how many things give off light. In the day-time, either these lights aren't on or you don't notice, but at night your observation skills will come into play.

Note down how many sources of light you can see.

Listen out for any noises around you, in the hedgerows, trees, fields, gardens, waste grounds, verges. When there's less light, your eyes aren't as useful, so your other senses become more important. Do you notice your hearing improves in the dark?

Note down how many sounds you hear and what you think they could be.

Sometimes you'll go out on a night-time walk and hear very little. Don't worry, there's always next time!

CHALLENGE

Try walking as quietly as you possibly can. The quieter you are, the more likely it is you'll have a night-time wildlife encounter. If you're quiet, you won't disturb the night-time world and may hear and see some interesting things! It's also a really fun challenge seeing if you can concentrate on every footstep and try to make it silent – it can be a fun game!

SLEEPING OUT

If you're lucky enough to have a garden, then that's the perfect place to try sleeping out for the first time. If you're a pro and have slept out a number of times already, then perhaps it's time for some camping a little further afield. However you choose to do it, here are a few simple tips to get you started.

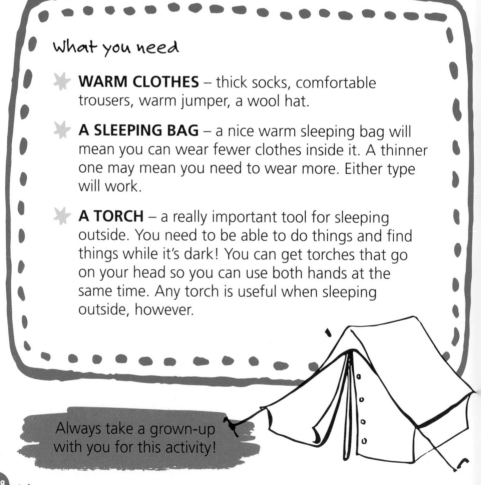

What you need

* **WARM CLOTHES** – thick socks, comfortable trousers, warm jumper, a wool hat.

* **A SLEEPING BAG** – a nice warm sleeping bag will mean you can wear fewer clothes inside it. A thinner one may mean you need to wear more. Either type will work.

* **A TORCH** – a really important tool for sleeping outside. You need to be able to do things and find things while it's dark! You can get torches that go on your head so you can use both hands at the same time. Any torch is useful when sleeping outside, however.

Always take a grown-up with you for this activity!

KEEPING DRY

A TENT – there are many different types of tent available, from family ones to small single-person tents. It depends what you're looking for and how much money you or your parents can spend. If there is a chance of rain, a tent is recommended!

A TARPAULIN – using a waterproof, plastic sheet or tarpaulin, you can create your very own tent. This is a cheap way to build a tent but will need help from an adult.

BIVI BAG – this is a waterproof bag that you pull over your sleeping bag, protecting it from any moisture like rain. It's a simple, quick way to keep yourself dry when sleeping outside and it's super fun! The great thing about a bivi bag is that you can lie down anywhere: on a hill, in the garden, in a field, in the woods, and while you're lying back you will be able to look right up at the stars in the night sky.

A SELF-BUILT SHELTER – one of the ultimate outdoor sleeping experiences is to build a shelter from material that you find in nature.

You could also sleep in a hammock (see pages 50–51).

Which outdoor sleeping methods have you used?

Tent ☐

Tarpaulin ☐

Self-built ☐

Bivi bag ☐

Hammock ☐

Other ☐

HAMMOCK LIFE

It's not only pirates on board their ships that sleep in hammocks. Sleeping in a hammock under the stars is becoming more and more popular and for very good reason – it's seriously good fun!

What to do

1 With the help of a grown-up, tie one end of the hammock to one of the trees, loosely at first around 1.5 m off the ground.

2 Tie the other end to the other tree and adjust the height on both until it's level.

3 Tie both ends tightly and securely.

You'll need:

* two trees, close enough together for a hammock to be hung
* a hammock
* a sleeping bag
* a camping mat (optional)

4 When it's time to sleep, climb into your sleeping bag first while on the ground, then sit in the hammock and swing your feet into it as you lie back.

5 Have a great sleep!

A hammock is a really exciting and comfortable way to sleep outdoors. If there's a chance of rain or it's particularly cold, tie a rope above your hammock and hang a waterproof tarpaulin over the rope. This will drape over you in your hammock and keep you sheltered from the rain. You can then hang a torch or battery-powered lantern from the rope above you, lie in your hammock, warm and dry off the ground, and read this book!

STAR GAZING

On a clear night there's nothing better to do than look up at the stars and wonder what's up there, thousands of miles away from your home on planet Earth. The night sky is fascinating and knowing a thing or two about it makes it even more interesting.

STARS

Stars are all around. They are enormous balls of hot gas that glow, allowing you to see them even though they are millions of miles away. You can see stars best when there are fewer clouds and in places where there is less human-made light. The middle of the countryside or on top of a mountain are usually good places, but you will still be able to see stars from towns and cities.

Throughout history, groups of stars have been given names and put into imaginary patterns in the sky. These are called constellations and are usually named after mythological creatures, people or animals. Knowing some of these gives you a reason to look up into the sky at night, to identify the stars and star patterns. Through history, constellations have been used in religion, as a measurement of time, for navigation, and particularly now for the science of astronomy.

Match each of the constellations names to the correct image.

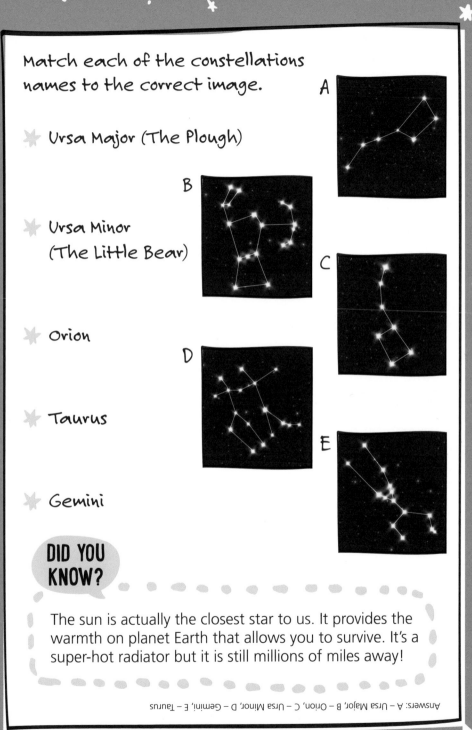

A

* Ursa Major (The Plough)

B

* Ursa Minor (The Little Bear)

C

* Orion

D

* Taurus

E

* Gemini

DID YOU KNOW?

The sun is actually the closest star to us. It provides the warmth on planet Earth that allows you to survive. It's a super-hot radiator but it is still millions of miles away!

Answers: A – Ursa Major, B – Orion, C – Ursa Minor, D – Gemini, E – Taurus

SATELLITES

Satellites are structures that go around the Earth, put in space by humans. This movement around the Earth is called an orbit, so satellites orbit the Earth.

Satellites are important for many different reasons. For example, satellites take pictures of other planets and space for scientists. Other satellites tell people about the weather, and allow them to communicate on the phone and through the internet.

A very important satellite is the International Space Station (ISS). The ISS orbits the Earth at about 5 miles per second, which is super-fast! This means that every 92 minutes it has been right around the Earth. It continuously orbits the Earth and will do so for many, many years to come. There are usually six astronauts living on board and their job is to study space, the Earth and understand how to live in space!

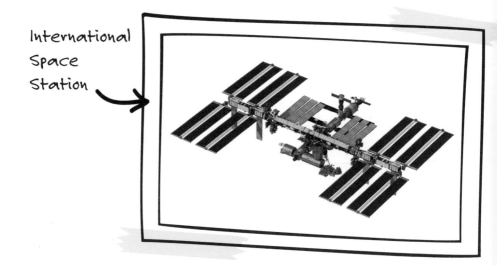

International Space Station

WHAT DO THEY LOOK LIKE?

Satellites move at a constant speed right across the sky. Sometimes they are faint and you can only just see them; others seem bigger and brighter and are easy to spot. Once you know what a satellite looks like, you'll be seeing them every time you look up!

What to do

1 Go outside after dark, find a really clear area of the sky as far away from lights as you can, and lie down on your back.

2 Look up into the sky and watch. Be really patient, look carefully, and you will see a satellite moving across the sky.

The ISS is best spotted by using an app on an adult's phone or by checking online to see what time it will be passing over your head. The information is very reliable and so, on a clear night, you can be sure to see it with your own eyes.

What time did you see the ISS?

Date _____

Time _____

THE MOON

The moon is a large natural satellite because it orbits the Earth. If you look closely and watch the moon over time, you will notice that it changes shape. The truth is it doesn't actually change shape, but it gets the shadow from Earth on it, which makes it look like it changes throughout the month.

Once a month you will see a 'full moon', which is where the moon is a perfect circle. Half-way between full moons (14 days), it will look like a thin sliver, which is called a 'crescent moon'.

Take this book outside at night-time. Look up at the moon, write down the date and draw what the moon looks like. Over the course of a week or two, you'll notice it change in shape.

You don't have to do this every day. Every few days will be enough, and you'll still notice a difference!

Date	Picture of the moon	Date	Picture of the moon

PLANETS

Five planets can be seen at night: Mercury, Venus, Mars, Jupiter and Saturn. They can be seen because they are closest to planet Earth in space. Remember though, they are still hundreds of millions of miles away! Some of these planets are more difficult to see than others and some can only be seen at certain times of the year.

It's really difficult to tell the difference between the planets and other stars, so unless you know exactly where they are in the night sky, you may not notice them. But look closely: Mars always looks slightly red, and Jupiter is often really bright! The next step is to get a telescope and start looking deeper into space.

Mercury

Venus

Saturn

Jupiter

Mars

WATER

Everything living on Earth needs water to survive, so it's very important to look after the water on the planet.

Water is essential, but it's also incredibly fun and can provide lots of entertainment and adventures! So, whether you're on, in or around a river, lake, the sea or a tiny pond, there's great fun to be had!

Wild water is something humans don't always know much about. This creates intrigue and interest when you're exploring this wet world! When you're near or in water, always keep your eyes open and note down what you see.

Jot down anything you notice!

WATER ACTIVITIES

- Litter picking
- Stone skimming
- Rock balancing

BE SAFE!

It's really important that you're with an adult at all times when near water.

FISHING

Catching fish is a skill used by people all over the world. There are many different ways to catch fish, but one of the easiest and most fun is to make your own rod and catch a fish in the traditional way.

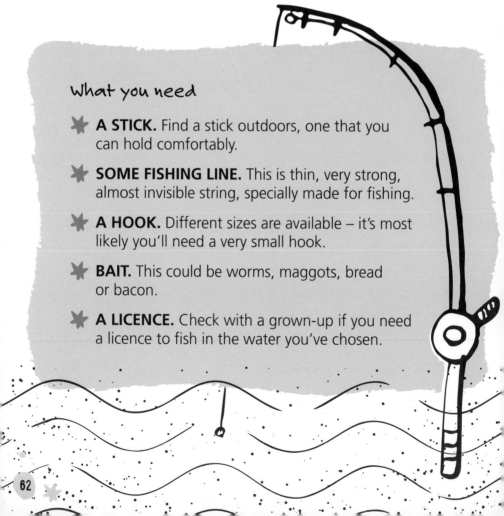

What you need

- ⭐ **A STICK.** Find a stick outdoors, one that you can hold comfortably.

- ⭐ **SOME FISHING LINE.** This is thin, very strong, almost invisible string, specially made for fishing.

- ⭐ **A HOOK.** Different sizes are available – it's most likely you'll need a very small hook.

- ⭐ **BAIT.** This could be worms, maggots, bread or bacon.

- ⭐ **A LICENCE.** Check with a grown-up if you need a licence to fish in the water you've chosen.

What to do

1 Tie the fishing line securely to the end of your rod.

2 Tie the hook onto the other end of the line. This must be very secure. Fishing hooks are extremely sharp, and the line is extremely thin. It's very tricky, so ask an adult to help you!

TIP!

Make sure the bait doesn't touch the bottom of the lake, pond or river, as fish rarely feed there.

3 Very carefully hook the bait onto the hook.

4 Throw the bait into the water and wait.

5 Every now and then pull your bait up. Check it's still on the hook and secure. Refresh it if needed.

6 When you feel a fish on the line, very gently pull the fish up out of the water. Sometimes the fish will escape, other times you'll be lucky!

7 Once you've caught the fish, very quickly unhook it and release it back into the water. Always return it to where it came from as quickly as possible.

Which fish?

Here are some common fish you may catch in cold water rivers and lakes. Which fish have you seen?

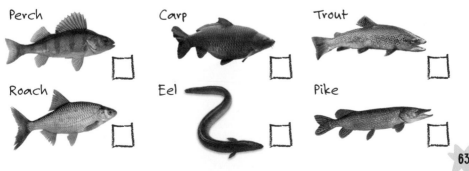

Perch ☐

Carp ☐

Trout ☐

Roach ☐

Eel ☐

Pike ☐

FISH TRAP

There is an easy way to catch small fish without using a fishing rod. You'll surprise your friends with this skill when you're out on an adventure together!

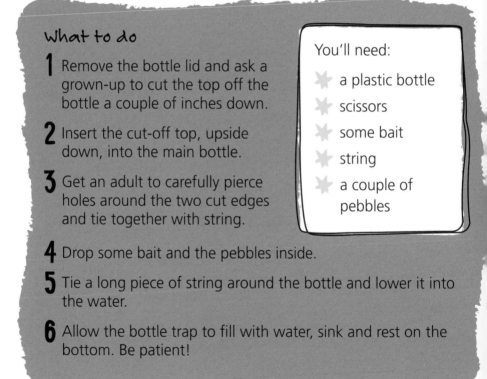

What to do

1 Remove the bottle lid and ask a grown-up to cut the top off the bottle a couple of inches down.

2 Insert the cut-off top, upside down, into the main bottle.

3 Get an adult to carefully pierce holes around the two cut edges and tie together with string.

4 Drop some bait and the pebbles inside.

5 Tie a long piece of string around the bottle and lower it into the water.

6 Allow the bottle trap to fill with water, sink and rest on the bottom. Be patient!

You'll need:

- ⭐ a plastic bottle
- ⭐ scissors
- ⭐ some bait
- ⭐ string
- ⭐ a couple of pebbles

If there are fish around, they will be attracted to the bait inside the bottle. Small fish will swim in through the opening, find the food but not be able to find their way out of the tiny opening they came through – they are trapped! It's a really fun and easy way to trap fish, but make sure you return the fish to the water once you're finished.

Did you trap any fish? Using page 63, can you identify the fish you caught? Draw a picture here.

BUILDING A DAM

Dam building is so much fun, have you ever tried it? The purpose of a dam is to stop water flowing, so when you're out exploring, and you find a small, shallow stream, why not have a go!

It will take a little work and time, you'll probably get cold hands and wet feet, but it will be something fun that you'll want to do again and again!

What to do

1 Lay some large rocks or branches in the stream from one side to the other.

2 Fill in any gaps with smaller rocks, pebbles, sticks and branches.

3 If there is mud and leaves, use them to try filling in any small gaps in the dam, to stop the water flowing.

You'll need:

* a small, shallow flowing stream
* rocks / branches
* wet mud / leaves
* wellington boots

4 This is great fun to do with a family member or a friend. You'll need to work together to stop the water flowing and plan how best to do this.

5 It's almost impossible to stop the water flowing completely in this way but notice what happens to the water when you build your dam.

6 Once you've finished your dam and it's time to leave, you must return the stream to its natural state. Leaving an obstruction in a stream can lead to serious problems such as flooding.

What do you notice?
Draw your dam here and
describe what happens
to the water.

WILD SWIMMING

Wild swimming has become really popular because it's so much fun! Most people usually swim in a warm pool but jumping into some cold outdoor water can be good for you!

BE SAFE!

It's important to have a grown-up with you when you're near water.

What to do

1 Very carefully get into the water and swim!

2 It's best to wear shoes when swimming outdoors. This helps you walk through any shallow parts, which may have sharp objects hidden underneath.

3 Keep an eye out for anything interesting you see. Wildlife is common around water.

You'll need:

* outdoor water – this could be a stream, pond or lake suitable for swimming in
* swimwear and swim shoes
* a little bit of courage!

4 A really fun challenge is to see if you can dive to the bottom and pick up a stone.

5 Cold water takes a while to get used to. To start with it may feel painful, but take your time, be patient and your body will adjust.

Keep a note of all the wild swimming locations you've swum at, even if it's just a dip!

Record what the water felt like, what you saw, and whether you would recommend this place to a friend.

RAFT BUILDING

What comes to mind when you hear the word raft? Someone shipwrecked escaping from a desert island? That's certainly one type of raft, but really a raft can be anything that you can float on! Rafts can be as simple or as complicated as you want to make them.

What to do

1 Securely tie together the plastic barrels with the string – strong, tight and secure. Ask a grown-up to help.

2 Lay the wooden pallet on top of the plastic barrels and secure that with string too.

3 You have a raft! Drag it to the water and launch your escape from Treasure Island – just don't forget to take a grown-up with you on your adventure...

You'll need:

* something that floats; for example, two plastic barrels with sealed lids

* a good amount of strong string or rope

* something to form a structure; for example, a wooden pallet

★ Rafts work best when they aren't too high out of the water. Fill the barrels with a little water if you need to keep the balance.

★ Rafts rely on symmetry. If there's one side longer or higher than the other it's likely the raft will topple and capsize, sending you flying into the water! Keep one side as similar to the other as possible.

BUILDING A POND

One of the very best ways to attract life to the place you live is to build a pond. Ponds, whatever their size, provide a habitat (place to live) for creatures that rely on water and also attract different species that use water. They are so much fun to build, amazing to watch and investigate, and are great for the environment, so give it a go!

What to do

1 Decide where your pond is going to go and either dig a hole to put your container in, or place it firmly and securely in position.

2 Cover the bottom with gravel and add some rocks.

3 Make sure there's a log or rock ramp coming out of the pond so an animal can climb out if it falls in.

4 Add your pond plants.

5 Fill with water – ideally use collected rainwater.

6 Leave your pond untouched for a few months and observe what happens.

You'll need:

- a watertight container; for example, an old sink, bucket or washing-up basin
- gravel and rocks
- pond plants – these can be bought from a garden centre

PONDLIFE

Your new pond will establish itself and become a little living world. The plants will grow and wildlife will be attracted to the habitat. You may find wildlife such as water boatmen, pond skaters, frogs, newts, dragonflies and mayfly larvae, and any number of other creatures could start to move in. If you're really lucky, hedgehogs may use the pond at night to drink from and you may find tadpoles in springtime. The pond will always be changing and becoming more and more interesting!

WADING

This is a simple adventure but one for the real explorers out there. There hasn't been an explorer in history who hasn't had to wade through some swamp, river or lake to discover a new kingdom. Why don't you head outside, prepare to get wet and become a real-life explorer?

WHAT IS WADING?

Wading is simply walking in water and exploring without actually swimming – your feet will always be on the ground. It can be done in shallow or deep water, as long as the water is not deeper than you!

What to do

1 Very carefully, step into the water and find your footing.

2 Walk through the water and enjoy discovering something new.

3 As you become more confident, you can go deeper. Remember, this is not swimming, so if it gets too deep, head back towards the land. Always go wading with a grown-up.

You'll need:

✺ a pond, river or lake that you'd really love to explore

✺ shoes that you don't mind getting wet

What did you observe as you explored the water?

ROCK POOLING

When you're next at the seaside, one of the best adventures you can have is to go rock pooling. All you need to get started is a bucket! Rock pooling is best done when the tide is at its lowest, so any holes, cracks or breaks in the rock will be exposed and leave a pool of seawater behind. In the pool, you will see a tiny little ocean world ready for you to explore!

What to do

1 At low tide, find a rock pool and look carefully into the water.

2 It's most likely you'll see creatures move. Take a moment and look at where they go and what they do. The more you look, the more you'll see.

3 Sea creatures are usually extremely well camouflaged, so when they move is the best time to spot them.

4 Dip your bucket into the water and see what you pull up.

5 Be sure to check under and amongst seaweed, which provides a great hiding place for many creatures!

6 Pick up any small rocks in the pool and see what's underneath.

7 Make sure you carefully return anything you find to the rock pool – it's their home!

Did you see any of these creatures?

Hermit crab ☐

Fish ☐

Sea snail ☐

Limpet ☐

Anemone ☐

Shrimp ☐

Other ☐

CRABBING

When you find yourself on a seaside adventure, one of the best things you can do is go crabbing!

What to do

1 Find a suitable location for crabbing. Sea walls and harbour walls are possible places. Check with a grown-up that it's a safe spot before you begin.

2 Put the bait inside the mesh bag and tie it to the line, close to the weight.

3 Lower the crab line into the water, allowing it to hit the bottom. Then wait.

4 Crabs have an amazing sense of smell underwater, so if there are crabs there it won't take long for them to arrive.

5 When you feel a crab on the line and it's started to feed, very carefully pull up the line.

6 Once it's out of the water, as quickly as you can, put the crab into the bucket and go again! Never forget to return the crabs to the sea when you're finished.

You'll need:

* a strong, thin crabbing line with a weight attached – you can buy these in many seaside locations or online

* bait – crabs are greedy things and love fish scraps or bacon

* a mesh washing-tablet bag

* a bucket

Record how many crabs you caught and find out what crabs most like to eat!

Bait	Number of crabs caught
Fish scraps	
Bacon	
Bread	
A bone	

NAVIGATION

Navigation (finding your way from one place to another) is a really useful skill. It's something that can help you right through life in many different situations, but learning and testing that skill can be an amazing adventure! There are loads of different ways to navigate. All we're trying to do is find out which way we're pointing: north, south, east or west.

A compass is something that tells you which way you are pointing. Compasses work because the Earth is magnetic and has something called a magnetic field.

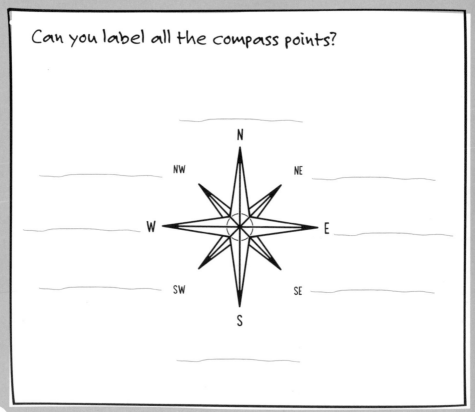

Can you label all the compass points?

N

NW   NE

W   E

SW   SE

S

MAKE A COMPASS

You can easily buy a compass but you can also make your own while you're outdoors.

What to do

1 Rub the magnet against the needle in the same direction about 20–30 times. Be careful, needles are sharp! This will magnetise the needle, turning it into a compass point.

2 Float the paper, cork or leaf on top of the water and carefully balance the needle on top. This is difficult and requires care.

You'll need:

✹ a needle

✹ a magnet

✹ a cup of water or a puddle

✹ a small piece of greaseproof paper, a small leaf or a small disc of cork

3 Your compass is complete! If the water is flat, the needle on the paper, cork or leaf will spin around and point towards the north or the south.

One end of the needle will be pointing north, the other south, but to be able to tell which is which, you'll have to piece together more clues using nature to help you.

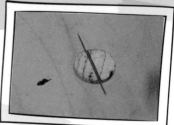

NATURAL NAVIGATION

THE SUN

The sun rises first thing in the morning in the east and sets last thing before night in the west. So, make sure you keep an eye on the sun and try to observe where it comes from and where it's going. That will give you another clue to add to the information gained from your very own compass.

THE TREES

Not only are trees incredibly awesome, but they can also help you find your way!

In the United Kingdom, the wind mostly blows from the south-west. So when you're out on an adventure and you see a tree growing in one direction looking like it's been pushed, have a think about which direction the wind may have been coming from. Because of this, trees, particularly on hills, quite often grow towards the north-east.

Now look closely at the leaves on a tree. Have you noticed that every leaf is slightly different? Leaves on the north side of a tree are usually smaller and thinner than leaves on the south side. This is because there is usually more light from the sun on the south side, so the leaves grow more.

Quite often moss grows more on the north side of the tree and doesn't grow on the south side. This is because the north side is wetter because the sun dries it out less, so the conditions are better for moss to grow.

THE STARS

Throughout history, the stars have been the main method used for navigation. To find north when it's dark, first you must find Ursa Major – The Plough (see page 53).

Looking straight up from the end of that star pattern you will see the North Star – Polaris. As long as it's a clear night, you will always be able to tell which way is north!

Have you noticed any of the features indicating direction during your adventures? Draw or note them down here.

GEOCACHING

Have you ever tried geocaching? If not, then it's time to start!

Geocaching is a fantastic way to start using your navigation skills and get yourself really thinking about the direction you're going in. It's a giant, world-wide treasure hunt which absolutely anyone can do. Using something called GPS coordinates, you will be directed to a place where you can then use your observation skills to find some hidden treasure – the geocache.

The geocache may be an object or a waterproof box with some interesting things inside. Each one is different – have a go and see what you can find!

What to do

1 Choose a geocache and type in the coordinates to your GPS.

2 Navigate towards the cache using the GPS device and your navigation skills.

3 Find the geocache, enjoy the treasure and search for a new one!

You'll need:

⭐ a GPS device or smartphone

⭐ an adult to register to the website: **geocaching.com**

What did you find while you were geocaching?

FLOUR TRAIL

It's often a good idea to turn your adventures into games that you can play with other people. Have you ever been on a treasure hunt? Well, how about if the treasure is another person! This is a simple, but fun and exciting way to have an outdoor adventure and you don't need much to do it – just a friend and a bag of flour. This is the flour trail adventure where you'll need all your tracking and observation skills!

Flour is a great marker material. The white will show up well but it's also a natural product that is biodegradable (decays naturally) and will do no harm to wildlife or the environment. Do be conscious of others though and only use small quantities at one time.

What to do

1 One person should set the trail (the trail setter), the other person / people are the hunters.

2 Give the trail setter a 5-minute head start.

3 The trail setter must drop small piles of flour every now and then as they make their way towards a hiding place.

4 This could be along the pavement, down the street, over the hills or through woodland. As long as the hunter(s) can find the flour marks, the hunt is on!

5 Only use a small amount of flour each time as a marker point. Don't make the mark too obvious, but similarly, don't hide it too well!

6 As the hunter finds each flour mark, they will get closer and closer to the trail setter, eventually finding their hiding place.

TIP!

If you're the trail setter, why not make decoy trails, where you go in one direction but then backtrack and lead the hunters in another direction. You can really confuse the hunters and have a lot of fun!

ADVENTURE COOKING

Don't tell the grown-ups but sometimes the very best meals you'll eat are cooked outside in the fresh air while on an adventure! For some reason food tastes great when you cook it over a fire you've made yourself. So like a real explorer in the wilderness, give outdoor cooking a go!

Make a list of food you'd like to try cooking outdoors.

FORAGING

Foraging is when you find food to eat while you're walking along. It's how our ancestors found food many thousands of years ago. It's how many tribespeople in remote parts of the world find food now.

BE SAFE!

It's important that the food you pick is safe to eat – always ask a grown-up to help you.

FRUIT – you may find a few different fruits growing wild but the most common is the blackberry. Blackberries grow on the spiky bramble plant and can be found everywhere. They are most plentiful around September / October. Blackberries are delicious and full of vitamins.

DANDELION – in springtime, there's a weed that grows everywhere. It has a bright yellow flower and it's called the dandelion. The leaves of the dandelion, when they are small and tender, make a great little salad. Wash the leaves well, then you'll have a natural, wild way to eat your greens!

Make sure you only pick dandelion leaves that are well away from humans or dogs; you don't want to be eating a dandelion after a dog has had a wee on it!

NUTS
(Do NOT collect nuts if you have a nut allergy.)

Hazelnut – it's really difficult to find nuts in the wild because the animals are usually one step ahead! Squirrels collect nuts by the thousands but if you're lucky to find some hazelnuts, then you'll have an amazing wild feast to enjoy. Hazelnuts are difficult to crack so you may need a rock or two to break the thick shell, but when you do you'll love them!

Beech nut – if you venture into a beech woodland in the autumn time, you'll be sure to see the ground covered in the shells of the beech nut. These are small, spiked shells and inside will be a number of seeds. If you peel the surface layer of the small seed you'll find a delicious nut inside. You'll need a lot to fill you up, but they are a great little woodland snack!

WILD GARLIC – it's really important to keep your senses open when you're on an outdoor adventure. Eyes to make sure you see all the exciting and interesting things, ears so you can hear everything, and smell – smell is often forgotten about, but sometimes it can be extremely useful. If you're walking along through the edge of a woodland and you smell a really strong garlic smell, stop and collect some of the green leaves at your feet. This will most likely be wild garlic and it's great to pop into a pot of food you're cooking over the fire!

FEAST IN A BAG

Spending time outside on an adventure can be exhausting! So when it comes to cooking we need something really nutritious and quick. These packets of food are so easy and delicious, you might be wanting to eat out every night of the year!

What to do

1 Ask a grown-up to help you light a fire, get it really hot, then don't add any more wood. Let it burn down so it's glowing gently.

2 While the fire is getting to the right stage, cut the vegetables into small chunks. Chop harder vegetables like carrots into small pieces and softer vegetables like courgette into bigger pieces.

3 Cut the chicken into small cubes (optional).

4 Lay the ingredients onto a sheet of tinfoil and cover in a drizzle of olive oil. You can add seasoning if you like.

5 Wrap it up in a package of foil, sealing the ingredients inside.

6 Put it straight onto the fire in amongst the red hot bits, or on a metal grate if you have one.

7 Leave for 30 minutes.

8 Ask a grown-up to very carefully remove from the heat and undo the tinfoil. Then enjoy one of the healthiest, most delicious meals cooked over a fire that you'll ever have!

You'll need:
- a small fire
- a roll of tinfoil
- olive oil
- a selection of vegetables, for example sweet potato, courgette, celery, tomato, pepper, carrots, parsnips
- a chicken breast (optional)
- a penknife

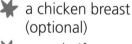

Here's a chance for you to add your favourite outdoor cooking ideas. What have you cooked, or what would your perfect adventure meal be?

TIP!

Why not add any nuts or wild garlic you found while foraging to the packet if it's the right time of year? A delicious addition!

BANANA PANCAKES

Banana pancakes are one of the easiest and most delicious things to cook outdoors while you're on an adventure. They're quick, simple and delicious!

What to do

1 Mash and mix the bananas with the eggs in the bowl.

2 Rest the frying pan on the embers of the fire, making sure it's flat and stable. Once the pan has heated up, pour in a little of the mixture. Get help from a grown-up for this bit.

3 Add some blackberries if it's the right time of year and you've been foraging.

4 Aim for small pancakes around 5 cm in diameter.

5 Cook for about a minute on one side then turn over the pancake using the spatula and cook the other side.

6 These pancakes do break up sometimes, but don't worry if they do – they will still be delicious!

7 After a couple of minutes of cooking they're ready to be taken off the heat and served up. Enjoy!

You'll need:

⭐ a small fire/stove

⭐ a frying pan

⭐ spatula

⭐ a bowl to mix the ingredients

⭐ 2 medium bananas

⭐ 2 eggs

Published by Collins
An imprint of HarperCollins Publishers
Westerhill Road, Bishopbriggs, Glasgow, G64 2QT

www.harpercollins.co.uk

© HarperCollins Publishers 2020

Collins ® is a registered trademark of HarperCollins Publishers Ltd.

Text © Alex Gregory
All images © Shutterstock.com
except: images on p.32, p.33; p.40(b); p.42(b) © HarperCollins Publishers

Publisher: Michelle I'Anson
Project manager: Rachel Allegro
Design: Sarah Duxbury
Typesetter: Jouve
Cover: Kevin Robbins

9780008372675

Printed in China

10 9 8 7 6 5 4 3 2 1